Theosophy and Social Justice

Also in this series:

Theosophy and the Search for Happiness
Texts by Moon Laramie and Annie Besant

Art and Theosophy
Texts by Martin Firrell and A.L. Pogosky

Theosophy and Esoteric Christianity
*Texts by Isis Resende, R. Heber Newton
& Franz Hartmann*

Theosophy and Yoga
Texts by Jenny Baker and Annie Besant

Forthcoming:

Theosophy and Clairvoyance
Texts by Kurt Leland and C.W. Leadbeater

The Purpose of Theosophy
Texts by Petra Meyer and Patience Sinnett

Theosophy and Social Justice

Texts by
Dr. Barbara B. Hebert,
William Quan Judge
& Annie Besant

martin firrell company
MODERN THEOSOPHY

First published in 2019 by Martin Firrell Company Ltd
10 Queen Street Place, London EC4R 1AG, United Kingdom.

ISBN 978-1-912622-17-7

Design © Copyright Martin Firrell Company 2019.
Introduction © Copyright Moon Laramie 2019.
Essay © Copyright Dr. Barbara B. Hebert 2019.

All rights reserved. No part of this publication may be reproduced, stored in or introduced into a retrieval system, or transmitted, in any form, or by any means (electronic, mechanical, photocopying, recording or otherwise) without the prior written consent of the publisher.

This book is sold subject to the condition that it shall not, by way of trade or otherwise, be lent, re-sold, hired out, or otherwise circulated without the publisher's prior consent in any form of binding or cover other than that in which it is published and without a similar condition including this condition being imposed on the subsequent purchaser.

Text is set in Baskerville, 12pt on 18pt.

Baskerville is a serif typeface designed in 1754 by John Baskerville (1706–1775) in Birmingham, England. Compared to earlier typeface designs, Baskerville increased the contrast between thick and thin strokes. Serifs were made sharper and more tapered, and the axis of rounded letters was placed in a more vertical position. The curved strokes were made more circular in shape, and the characters became more regular.

Baskerville is categorised as a transitional typeface between classical typefaces and high contrast modern faces. Of his own typeface, John Baskerville wrote, 'Having been an early admirer of the beauty of letters, I became insensibly desirous of contributing to the perfection of them. I formed to myself ideas of greater accuracy than had yet appeared, and had endeavoured to produce a set of types according to what I conceived to be their true proportion.'

Introduction
by Moon Laramie

In this edition of the *Modern Theosophy* series, Dr. Barbara B. Hebert, Annie Besant and William Quan Judge explore the relationship between theosophy and social justice. William Quan Judge takes the view that 'it is for us to follow the line of action which shall result first in harmony now and forever, and second, in the reduction of the general sum of hate and opposition in thought or act which now darkens the world.'

US President Barack Obama's 2009 speech at Cairo University echoed this sentiment: 'Recognising our common humanity is only the beginning of our task. Words alone cannot meet the needs of our people. These needs will be met only if we act boldly in the years ahead; and if we understand that the challenges we face are shared, and our failure to meet them will hurt us all.'[1]

In his book, *Non-Violence or Non-Existence*, the Indian British social activist Satish Kumar comments that, 'Almost every moment sees someone somewhere dying of starvation. What right have we to waste our human resources on weapons of destruction? The real enemy is fear and mistrust.'[2]

A rejection of such mistrust coupled with the concept of universal brotherhood is something which lies at the heart of the theosophical tradition. Barbara Hebert observes that 'as theosophists we are willing to walk this rocky path towards conscious awareness of who we are and of the unity of all life'. It is this sense of unity which, she argues, is central to the development of social justice: 'To be a social activist is to walk the spiritual path whether a person knows it or not... They are serving all of humanity or the animal kingdom and the environment. They are uplifting all which is the goal. That is the spiritual path.' Similarly, Satish Kumar describes his belief in 'a new form of community living based on spirituality and human relationship',[3] an idea first posited by the political ethicist Mahatma Gandhi. Annie Besant takes this a step further, identifying the role she feels spirituality has to play at a national level: 'Religion in National Life shows how spiritual traditions have shaped our attitudes towards each other and towards justice and altruism… Nations growing over-wealthy and over-luxurious tend to lose acuteness of intellect, and still more to lose the keenness of spiritual insight.'

In his article *Is Poverty Bad Karma?*, William Quan Judge explores the question of karma in relation to extreme poverty: 'Does it follow, because a man is born in the lowest station in life, compelled always to live in the humblest way, often starving and hearing his wife and children cry out for food, that therefore he is suffering from bad karma?' Judge believes this cannot be the case: 'These egos… are voluntarily, for all we know, going through that difficult school so as to acquire further deep experience and with it strength.' Barbara Hebert emphasises that using karma as an excuse to absolve ourselves of responsibility towards others is not the theosophical path: 'Theosophy is the practice of altruism. If we act altruistically, we put the needs of the whole before the needs of the self. When we realise the unity of all, we realise that what happens to one of us, happens to all of us. We are the Rohingya,[4] we are the hungry, we are the children who live in war-torn countries, we are refugees. We are the other, whoever that is.'

For the modern theosophist, it is altruism based on unity consciousness which provides the foundation for social justice. As William Quan Judge observes, 'The un-theosophical view is based on separation, the Theosophical upon unity absolute and actual. Of course if Theosophists talk of unity but as a dream or a mere metaphysical thing, then they will cease to be Theosophists'.

1. Barack Obama, speech, Cairo University, 4 June 2009.

2. *Non-Violence or Non-Existence*, Satish Kumar, Christian Action Publications, 1969.

3. Ibid.

4. The Rohingya people are a stateless Indo-Aryan ethnic group who reside in Rakhine State, Myanmar (previously known as Burma).

Dr. Barbara B. Hebert

Dr. Barbara Bradley Hebert is the President of the Theosophical Society in America (TSA).

Born in Covington, Louisiana, she is a third-generation theosophist and has been a member of the TSA since 1976.

From the mid-1970s to the mid-1980s, she worked on the staffs of the National Headquarters, Olcott, in Wheaton, Illinois, and the Krotona Institute of Theosophy in Ojai, California. She later served on the TSA's national Board of Directors.

She has been active in local, regional, and national theosophical activities. Throughout the years, she has worked as a mental health professional and educator in a variety of settings.

She cites the theosophical texts that have most influenced her as Jiddu Krishnamurti's *At the Feet of the Master* and H.P. Blavatsky's *The Voice of the Silence*. Both books, she says, always enable the reader to learn something new and gain greater insight into the self and the world.

Theosophy and Social Justice
by Dr. Barbara B. Hebert (2019)

These days, social justice is a term thrown around very easily by any number of people in social media and elsewhere. It's a huge concept that applies to many of society's problems and, as we all know, society has plenty of problems. Before we go any further, it's important to understand the meaning of this concept. The word 'social' obviously relates to society which is the aggregate of all people who live. It is the aggregate of all of them together - the unity of individuals. From the perspective of the perennial wisdom, we can expand this definition even further and talk about the aggregate of all living beings, of all life. At the deepest level, all of us are one. From this perspective then, 'society' includes everything. 'Justice' means equality, fairness, equity, all of us having the same privileges, the same opportunities, the same responsibilities. No one is treated differently. All are treated fairly and impartially.

When we put the two together to form the idea of 'social justice', we are talking about fairness and equity for all living things. Social justice is equity and fairness for humans, animals, nature, Mother Earth, our solar system, our galaxy, our universe and beyond. This is because we are all connected. The idea of social justice has a central place in the theosophical worldview because the first object of the Theosophical Society focuses on unity and the unity of all life. Therefore, from a theosophical perspective, social justice applies across the board, not just to human beings.

If we are all one, then what happens to one of us, happens to all of us. If one person is treated unfairly, we are all treated unfairly. If we don't care for our mother, the earth, then we are not caring for ourselves because we *are* that mother. When we leave junk in space, we're contaminating ourselves because the solar system is us. Whatever happens to me happens to you and vice versa. This is the very core of the esoteric doctrine.

Perhaps from the standpoint of spirituality and the perennial wisdom, we need to add another component - compassion. This is a strong feeling for the suffering of others and a desire to help. We must add compassion when we talk about social justice. From this perspective, social justice is the spiritual path. Spiritual evolution, self-transformation, and awakening walk hand in hand with compassion for others. Selfless concern for the wellbeing of others is one way of starting out on the spiritual path. Working for the welfare of others, with a deep sense of compassion, means that all beings are uplifted. All have the same opportunities so that life in its varied forms is honored and respected.

Whether a person knows it or not, to be a social activist is to walk the spiritual path. There are many people in the world who are unaware that they are walking this path to spiritual unfoldment but as long as they have that compassion for others and they work to help uplift them, they are undoubtedly walking this path. They are serving all of humanity or the animal kingdom and the environment. They are uplifting all and this is the goal. This is the spiritual path.

It is difficult to gain an awareness of the unity of the whole and of our place in the universe. It's difficult to re-awaken what is already inherent in us but of which we are not necessarily conscious. It is a rocky path and it can be very hard. Working for social justice requires courage. But as theosophists we are willing to walk this rocky path towards conscious awareness of who we are and of the essential unity of all life.

What role does karma play? This is not an easy question to answer. People have written many books on the subject of karma but few of us truly understand it. Those of us who have studied the perennial wisdom have a degree of insight. Karma is implicated in the action of helping others. How do our actions relate to our own karma or the karma of other people, or animals, or nature, whoever or whatever we are trying to help? Though our understanding is limited, karma must still be taken into account in any discussion of social justice and social activism.

Karma is frequently referred to as the Law of Cause and Effect or the Law of Action and Reaction. When I was a child I used to think: if I hit my sister, I will end up in the next life with a sister who is going to hit me. It's pretty simplistic but it was my understanding: if I did this thing, then that thing would happen. Over the years my perspective has changed. My understanding of karma at this point in my life (and this may change with further study) is that it is a universal law based on harmony. Everything we think, say, and do impacts the harmony of the universe and this law works to restore that harmony. H.P. Blavatsky writes, 'Karma creates nothing, nor does it design. It is the individual who plans and creates causes, and Karmic Law adjusts the effects; which adjustment is not an act, but universal harmony, tending ever to resume its original position, like a bough, which, bent down too forcibly, rebounds with corresponding vigour.'[1]

When we pull the branch down, we disturb the harmony of the tree and when we let go, it springs back up so that it can find its place again in harmony. So it's not about hitting my sister and ending up with a sister who hits me. It's about harmony and balance in the universe. Today, people talk about karma freely but they often take a simplistic view of it. People will often say that if you do something bad, then 'karma is going to get you!' Karma is found in many religious and spiritual traditions. In the West, we commonly think of it as an 'eastern' concept but it is also implied in the writings of Christianity and Judaism. For example, in Galatians, Paul says, 'Whatsoever a man soweth, that shall he also reap.' In the Old Testament,

Hosea[2] prophesies about Israel, saying, 'For they sow the wind and they shall reap the whirlwind.'

The American Tibetan Buddhist Pema Chödrön[3] said, 'The idea of karma is that you continually get the teaching you need to open your heart.' We think of karma as being about bad things that happen to us, but karma is not just about balance. Within that balance, karma teaches us. Positive or negative, everything that happens to us is a lesson. It's there to teach us to open our hearts. As theosophists, we believe we are on the earth to learn and grow. We are here to transform spiritually so it makes sense that our life circumstances facilitate this process. We are reminded in some of the theosophical writings that karma's workings are not mechanistic and are difficult to predict even by those self-actualized beings frequently referred to as the Mahatmas.

In Letter 126 of *The Mahatma Letters*, Koot Hoomi tells A.P. Sinnett: 'You know nothing of the ins and outs of the work of Karma… Have another look at Karma, ponder over the above, and remember that it ever works in the most unexpected ways.' While we think we understand karma, what we perceive may not be entirely accurate. It is helpful to look at this universal law in light of social justice. For example, if someone is born into a marginalized culture that does not have equal rights or opportunities, we might say this is a result of their karma. We might say that they are supposed to learn something from the experience so we don't have the right to change it. We don't have the right to alter somebody's karma.

Annie Besant was the second President of the Theosophical Society and was an influential social activist in her own right. Annie Besant said, 'You need not be troubled about Karma any more than by the law of gravitation. You cannot interfere with it. Sometimes you find (a person) who says, 'I must not help so and so; it is his/her Karma to suffer.' You might as well say you will not pick up a child that has fallen because, by the law of gravitation, it has fallen and must be left under its law to take care of itself. Your duty is to do all you can to help others. Do not take Karma as an excuse for indolence.'[4] If somebody trips and falls, then you should help them get back on their feet. Gravity doesn't mean that person has to stay there.

If we remember that we are all one in the truest sense of the word, then we can reflect on these words of the Mahatma Morya to H.P. Blavatsky: 'Do not be ever thinking of yourself and forgetting that there are others; for you have no karma of your own, but the karma of each one is the karma of all.' We are connected. William Quan Judge wrote, 'Karmic causes already set in motion must be allowed to sweep on until exhausted but this permits no person to refuse to help others and every sentient being.'[5] He also says, 'We should not shrink from the duty to relieve pain and sorrow if we can. For it is both cowardice and conceit to say that we will not help this or that person because it is his or her karma to suffer. In the face of suffering it is our good karma to relieve it if it is in our power.'[6]

This brings us to dharma. In the West, dharma is not referred to as often as karma but it is still quite well known. It has been called 'responsibility' or 'duty'. For a long time, I thought that my dharma was to be a mother and raise my children. That is probably the case to some extent, as I learned a lot about myself through that process, as does any parent. But my understanding of dharma at that point in my life was minimal and simplistic. Just like other metaphysical concepts, dharma is very complex and can be interpreted in many ways. In this instance, we are talking about dharma in a theosophical context. My understanding is that dharma means living according to the law of spiritual evolution. Joy Mills writes that 'dharma is our inevitable destiny', the rightness of our self-becoming nature, becoming real and one with all that is. Dharma from this perspective is the path of spiritual unfoldment.

We live our dharma when we work toward an understanding of our true nature, the magnificence of our higher selves and our essential unity with all life. Our dharma is our duty, our responsibility to make choices - in thoughts, words and actions - that move us toward our ultimate destiny as self-actualized human beings. The lotus flower is symbolic of who we are. It is rooted in the mud and silt of murky water. It works its way up through this murky water until it finally emerges on the surface and there it blooms in the light. This happens even though its root is still submerged in the mud. Its full beauty is realized through this journey. Similarly, the beauty of the higher aspect of ourselves is realized through a journey that frequently begins in the murky and muddy existence that we call life. We are always growing up toward the light so that we can blossom into beauty.

Both karma and dharma, if understood at a deeper level, leave us no choice but to become social activists. As has been stated by many throughout the years, theosophy is the practice of altruism. The Australian theosophist and educator Dorothy Bell[7] said, 'As a principle, altruism expresses the true root meaning of the words 'theos' and 'Brahma' - the motion of outward expansion from within… It means giving outwardly and unconditionally to the whole from within. It realizes the wholeness and unity of all. And every movement of that realization of wholeness is open and generous and all-embracing. It is compassion, love, gentleness, kindness, and the full expression of who we truly are.' If we act altruistically, we put the needs of the whole before the needs of the self. When we realize the unity of all, we realize that what happens to one of us, happens to all of us. We are the Rohingya,[8] we are the hungry, we are the children who live in war-torn countries, we are refugees. We are the other, whoever that is.

There are as many methods of social activism as there are people. We all have to choose our own direction based on what's inside us. We have to be guided by our own concerns and passions. The Theosophical Society as an organization does not take a stand on any issue beyond those associated with its three objects - unity and reverence for all life; open-minded enquiry into religion, philosophy and science; and spiritual self-transformation. The society has no dogma. Members are not required to believe any one thing. They have only to be in sympathy with the society's three objects. The society does not adopt a particular position. It is up to individual members to decide if and how they want to take a stand. Personally, I believe we are compelled to become social activists and seek social justice for everyone.

There are outer ways and inner ways of serving. Outer ways include protesting, becoming involved with politics, becoming involved in charitable activities and projects. There is social need everywhere and we can get involved practically and do something to address it. These outer ways of serving others are very valuable. There are also inner ways of serving. One of the basic teachings in the theosophical body of literature is that thought has power. When we send out thoughts of peace, love and compassion, they radiate around the world. We are sending out peace and compassion when we meditate on world peace or on alleviating the suffering of others. Becoming self-aware is another way to serve the world because as we change, everyone else changes. What happens to one happens to all. When one of us makes the tiniest movement towards awakening awareness within, all of us are moved a tiny bit further in that direction. Changing ourselves changes the world.

Dorothy Bell shared the story of a woman she knew called Maria. Maria felt a great affinity with the theosophical worldview. But, to Maria, seeing the one life in all creation seemed vague and abstract. Even so, she felt the idea was very compelling and decided to work on it in her daily life. She would look at a tree, person, or animal and she would say to herself, 'That is an expression of the one life.' This is reminiscent of Sri Ram's words in his book *Consciousness, Its Nature and Action*.[9] He wrote, 'Life is nothing but consciousness completely conditioned by the organism it uses.' Maria even called her cat 'God-Cat' to remind her of the inner reality obscured by the outer physical form. She spent months training her mind in this way but, despite these efforts, she was still struggling to experience the truth that all life is a unity. One day, she was walking along a busy city street. A homeless man appeared out of a shadowy side alley and stepped into her path. He was bearded, long-haired, wild-eyed and dirty. Maria's initial reaction was repulsion, disgust, some fear, and a little anger. But, as she began to turn away, a strong thought stopped her: 'This is the one life expressing itself in this man.' She was stunned. She saw the man in this new light, grasping the sacredness of his journey on this planet. The disgust and fear disappeared. She felt nothing specific towards him as a person, only a general sense of goodwill and freedom. Later, when she shared her story, someone said, 'But you didn't give him anything.' She thought about it and then she said, 'I did. I gave him respect.'

However we change ourselves, we are

changing the world. What happens to one, happens to all. We must be social activists. We must advocate for social justice in our world in our own way, whether outwardly, inwardly or both. It is not just our karma to do it, it is our dharma. It is part of walking this path. As our candle is lit, so are the candles of every other. To paraphrase Helen Keller:[10] 'Social justice will be attained when the great mass of people are filled with the sense of responsibility for each other's welfare.'

1. Helena Petrovna Blavatsky, *The Secret Doctrine, Vol. II.*

2. Hosea (meaning 'salvation' or 'He saves' or 'He helps'), son of Beeri, was an 8th-century BC prophet in Israel who authored the book of prophecies bearing his name. He is one of the Twelve Prophets of the Jewish Hebrew Bible, also known as the Minor Prophets of the Christian Old Testament. Hosea is often seen as a 'prophet of doom' but underneath his message of destruction is a promise of restoration. The Talmud claims that he was the greatest prophet of his generation. The period of Hosea's ministry extended to some sixty years, and in his time, he was the only prophet of Israel to leave written prophecy.

3. Pema Chödrön (born Deirdre Blomfield-Brown 14 July 1936) is an American Tibetan Buddhist. She is an ordained nun, acharya (religious instructor) and disciple of the Buddhist meditation master, Chögyam Trungpa Rinpoche. Chödrön has written several dozen books and audiobooks and is principal teacher at Gampo Abbey in Nova Scotia, Canada.

4. Annie Besant, *Theosophical Lectures*, Rajput Press, 1907

5. William Quan Judge, *Aphorisms on Karma, The Path*, March 1893

6. William Quan Judge, *Men Karmic Agents, The Path*, March 1892

7. Dorothy Bell is a member of the Theosophical Society in Australia, serving on the national executive committee and education unit. She has given theosophical programmes and published articles internationally. She joined the Theosophical Society in 1999.

8. The Rohingya people are a stateless Indo-Aryan ethnic group who reside in Rakhine State, Myanmar (previously known as Burma).

9. Nilakanta Sri Ram (15 December 1889 - 8 April 1973) was an Indian theosophist who served from 1953-1973 as the fifth

International President of the Theosophical Society based in Adyar, Chennai, India. He was much loved as a teacher, lecturer, and writer.

10. Helen Adams Keller (27 June 1880 – 1 June 1968) was an American author, political activist, and lecturer. She was the first deaf-blind person to earn a Bachelor of Arts degree. The story of Keller and her teacher, Anne Sullivan, was made famous by Keller's autobiography, *The Story of My Life*, and its adaptations for film and stage. A member of the Socialist Party of America and the Industrial Workers of the World, she campaigned against militarism and for women's suffrage and workers' rights.

William Quan Judge

William Quan Judge was born on 13 April 1851 in Dublin, Ireland, emigrating to the United States when he was 13. He was an Irish-American mystic and esotericist and one of the founders of the original Theosophical Society.

A vigorous, imaginative, and idealistic young man, he was among the 17 people who established the Theosophical Society.

When Henry Steel Olcott and Helena Blavatsky left the United States for India, Judge stayed behind to manage the society's work, while also continuing his career as a lawyer.

In 1886, Judge established *The Path*, an independent theosophical magazine. His natural interest in the welfare of others informed everything he did. His articles and theosophical talks are expressed in the idiomatic language of the common man.

William Quan Judge died on 21 March 1896 in New York City.

Is Poverty Bad Karma?
by William Quan Judge (1891)

The question of what is good karma and what bad has been usually considered by theosophists from a very worldly and selfish standpoint. The commercial element has entered into the calculation as to the result of merit and demerit.

Eternal Justice, which is but another name for karma, has been spoken of as awarding this or that state of life to the reincarnating ego solely as a mere balance of accounts in a ledger, with a payment in one case by way of reward and a judgment for debt in another by way of punishment.

It has been often thought that if a man be rich and well circumstanced it must follow that in his prior incarnation he was good although poor; and that if he now be in poverty the conclusion is that, when on earth before, his life was bad if rich. So it has come about that the sole test of good or bad karma is one founded entirely upon his purse. But is poverty with all its miseries bad karma?

Does it follow, because a man is born in the lowest station in life, compelled always to live in the humblest way, often starving and hearing his wife and children cry out for food, that therefore he is suffering from bad karma?

If we look at the question entirely from the plane of this one life, this personality, then of course what is disagreeable and painful in life may be said to be bad. But if we regard all conditions of life as experiences undergone by the ego for the purpose of development, then even poverty ceases to be 'bad karma'. Strength comes only through trial and exercise.

In poverty are some of the greatest tests for endurance, the best means for developing the strength of character which alone leads to greatness. These egos, then, whom we perceive around us encased in bodies whose environment is so harsh that endurance is needed to sustain the struggle, are voluntarily, for all we know, going through that difficult school so as to acquire further deep experience and with it strength.

The old definition of what is good and what bad karma is the best. That is: 'Good karma is that which is pleasing to Ishvara, and bad that which is displeasing to Ishvara.'[1]

There is here but very little room for dispute as to poverty or wealth; for the test and measure are not according to our present evanescent human tastes and desires, but are removed to the judgment of the immortal self-Ishvara. The self may not wish for the pleasures of wealth, but seeing the necessity for discipline decides to assume life among mortals in that low station where endurance, patience, and strength may be acquired by experience. There is no other way to implant in the character the lessons of life.

It may then be asked if all poverty and low condition are good karma? This we can answer, under the rule laid down, in the negative. Some such lives, indeed many of them, are bad karma, displeasing to the immortal self imprisoned in the body, because they are not by deliberate choice, but the result of causes blindly set in motion in previous lives, sure to result in planting within the person the seeds of wickedness that must later be uprooted with painful effort.

Under this canon, then, we would say that the masses of poor people who are not bad in nature are enduring oftener than not good karma, because it is in the line of experience Ishvara has chosen, and that only those poor people who are wicked can be said to be suffering bad karma, because they are doing and making that which is displeasing to the immortal self within.

1. Ishvara is a concept in Hinduism, with a wide range of meanings that depend on the era and the school of Hinduism. In ancient texts of Indian philosophy, depending on the context, Ishvara can mean supreme soul, ruler, lord, king, queen or husband. In medieval era Hindu texts, depending on the school of Hinduism, Ishvara means God, supreme being, personal god, or special self. In Shaivism and for many Hindus, Ishvara is synonymous with 'Shiva', sometimes as Maheshvara or Parameshvara meaning the 'supreme lord', or as an Ishtadeva (personal god). Similarly for Vaishnavists and many Hindus, it is synonymous with Vishnu. In traditional Bhakti movements, Ishvara is one or more deities of an individual's preference from Hinduism's polytheistic canon of deities. In modern sectarian movements such as Arya Samaj and Brahmoism, Ishvara takes the form of a monotheistic God. In the Yoga school of Hinduism, it is any 'personal deity' or 'spiritual inspiration'. In the Advaita Vedanta school, Ishvara is a monistic universal absolute that connects and is the oneness in everyone and everything.

How Should We Treat Others?
by William Quan Judge (1896)

The subject relates to our conduct toward and treatment of our fellows, including in that term all people with whom we have any dealings. No particular mode of treatment is given by Theosophy. It simply lays down the law that governs us in all our acts, and declares the consequences of those acts. It is for us to follow the line of action which shall result first in harmony now and forever, and second, in the reduction of the general sum of hate and opposition in thought or act which now darkens the world.

The great law which Theosophy first speaks of is the law of karma, and this is the one which must be held in view in considering the question. Karma is called by some the 'law of ethical causation', but it is also the law of action and reaction; and in all departments of nature the reaction is equal to the action, and sometimes the reaction from the unseen but permanent world seems to be much greater than the physical act or word would appear to warrant on the physical plane.

This is because the hidden force on the unseen plane was just as strong and powerful as the reaction is seen by us to be. The ordinary view takes in but half of the facts in any such case and judges wholly by superficial observation.

If we look at the subject only from the point of view of the person who knows not of Theosophy and of the nature of man, nor of the forces Theosophy knows to be operating all the time, then the reply to the question will be just the same as the everyday man makes. That is, that he has certain rights he must and will and ought to protect; that he has property he will and may keep and use any way he pleases; and if a man injure him he ought to and will resent it; that if he is insulted by word or deed he will at once fly not only to administer punishment on the offender, but also try to reform, to admonish, and very often to give that offender up to the arm of the law; that if he knows of a criminal he will denounce him to the police and see that he has meted out to him the punishment provided by the law of man.

Thus in everything he will proceed as is the custom and as is thought to be the right way by those who live under the Mosaic retaliatory law.[1]

But if we are to inquire into the subject as Theosophists, and as Theosophists who know certain laws and who insist on the absolute sway of karma, and as people who know what the real constitution of man is, then the whole matter takes on, or ought to take on, a wholly different aspect.

The untheosophical view is based on separation, the Theosophical upon unity absolute and actual. Of course if Theosophists talk of unity but as a dream or a mere metaphysical thing, then they will cease to be Theosophists, and be mere professors, as the Christian world is today, of a code not followed. If we are separate one from the other the world is right and resistance is a duty, and the failure to condemn those who offend is a distinct breach of propriety, of law, and of duty. But if we are all united as a physical and psychical fact, then the act of condemning, the fact of resistance, the insistence upon rights on all occasions - all of which means the entire lack of charity and mercy - will bring consequences as certain as the rising of the sun tomorrow.

What are those consequences, and why are they?

They are simply this, that the real man, the entity, the thinker, will react back on you just exactly in proportion to the way you act to him, and this reaction will be in another life, if not now, and even if now felt will still return in the next life.

The fact that the person whom you condemn, or oppose, or judge seems now in this life to deserve it for his acts in this life, does not alter the other fact that his nature will react against you when the time comes. The reaction is a law not subject to nor altered by any sentiment on your part. He may have, truly, offended you and even hurt you, and done that which in the eye of man is blameworthy, but all this does not have anything to do with the dynamic fact that if you arouse his enmity by your condemnation or judgment there will be a reaction on you, and consequently on the whole of society in any century when the reaction takes place. This is the law and the fact as given by the Adepts, as told by all sages, as reported by those who have seen the inner side of nature, as taught by our philosophy and easily provable by anyone who will take the trouble to examine carefully. Logic and small facts of one day or one life, or arguments on lines laid down by men of the world who do not know the real power and place of thought nor the real nature of man cannot sweep this away. After all argument and logic it will remain. The logic used against it is always lacking in certain premises based on facts, and while seeming to be good logic, because the missing facts are unknown to the logician, it is false logic. Hence an appeal to logic that ignores facts which we know are certain is of no use in this inquiry. And the ordinary argument always uses a number of assumptions which are destroyed by the actual inner facts about thought, about karma, about the reaction by the inner man.

The Master K.H.[2] once writing to Mr. Sinnett in *The Occult World*, and speaking for his whole order and not for himself only, distinctly wrote that the man who goes to denounce a criminal or an offender works not with nature and harmony but against both, and that such act tends to destruction instead of construction. Whether the act be large or small, whether it be the denunciation of a criminal, or only your own insistence on rules or laws or rights, does not alter the matter or take it out of the rule laid down by that Adept. For the only difference between the acts mentioned is a difference of degree alone; the act is the same in kind as the violent denunciation of a criminal. Either this Adept was right or wrong. If wrong, why do we follow the philosophy laid down by him and his messenger, and concurred in by all the sages and teachers of the past? If right, why this swimming in an adverse current, as he said himself, why this attempt to show that we can set aside karma and act as we please without consequences following us to the end of time? I know not. I prefer to follow the Adept, and especially so when I see that what he says is in line with facts in nature and is a certain conclusion from the system of philosophy I have found in Theosophy.

I have never found an insistence on my so-called rights at all necessary. They preserve themselves, and it must be true if the law of karma is the truth that no man offends against me unless I in the past have offended against him.

In respect to man, karma has no existence without two or more persons being considered. You act, another person is affected, karma follows. It follows on the thought of each and not on the act, for the other person is moved to thought by your act. Here are two sorts of karma, yours and his, and both are intermixed. There is the karma or effect on you of your own thought and act, the result on you of the other person's thought; and there is the karma on or with the other person consisting of the direct result of your act and his thoughts engendered by your act and thought. This is all permanent. As affecting you there may be various effects. If you have condemned, for instance, we may mention some: (a) the increased tendency in yourself to indulge in condemnation, which will remain and increase from life to life; (b) this will at last in you change into violence and all that anger and condemnation may naturally lead to; (c) an opposition to you is set up in the other person, which will remain forever until one day both suffer for it, and this may be in a tendency in the other person in any subsequent life to do you harm and hurt you in the million ways possible in life, and often also unconsciously. Thus it may all widen out and affect the whole body of society. Hence no matter how justifiable it may seem to you to condemn or denounce or punish another, you set up cause for sorrow in the whole race that must work out some day. And you must feel it.

The opposite conduct, that is, entire charity, constant forgiveness, wipes out the opposition from others, expends the old enmity and at the same time makes no new similar causes. Any other sort of thought or conduct is sure to increase the sum of hate in the world, to make cause for sorrow, to continually keep up the crime and misery in the world. Each man can for himself decide which of the two ways is the right one to adopt.

Self-love and what people call self-respect may shrink from following the Adept's view I give above, but the Theosophist who wishes to follow the law and reduce the general sum of hate will know how to act and to think, for he will follow the words of the Master of H.P.B. who said: 'Do not be ever thinking of yourself and forgetting that there are others; for you have no karma of your own, but the karma of each one is the karma of all.' And these words were sent by H.P.B. to the American Section and called by her words of wisdom, as they seem also to me to be, for they accord with law. They hurt the personality of the 19th Century, but the personality is for a day, and soon it will be changed if Theosophists try to follow the law of charity as enforced by the inexorable law of karma. We should all constantly remember that if we believe in the Masters we should at least try to imitate them in the charity they show for our weakness and faults. In no other way can we hope to reach their high estate, for by beginning thus we set up a tendency which will one day perhaps bring us near to their development; by not beginning we put off the day forever.

1. 'An eye for an eye' or the law of retaliation is the principle that a person who has injured another person should be penalized to a similar degree, and the person inflicting such punishment should be the injured party. In softer interpretations, it means the victim receives the estimated value of the injury in compensation.

2. K.H. is an abbreviation of Koot Hoomi (also spelled Kuthumi), one of the Mahatmas that inspired the founding of the Theosophical Society in 1875.

Annie Besant

Annie Besant was born in London on 1 October 1847. She was a women's rights activist, supporter of Irish independence, socialist, author and was president of the Theosophical Society from 1907 until her death in 1933. In 1867, she married Frank Besant, a clergyman, and they had two children. However, her criticism of his political and religious views led to their legal separation in 1873. She then became an active member of the National Secular Society (NSS). In 1877, she helped publish a book, *Fruits of Philosophy* by Charles Knowlton, the American birth control campaigner. The ensuing scandal put her in the public spotlight. Besant was a prolific writer and initially wrote a weekly column in *The National Reformer.* In her articles she argued for Irish home rule and a secular state in Britain. Later Besant became involved with social justice campaigns, including the London match girls strike of 1888. She was a prominent speaker for the Fabian Society and the Marxist Social Democratic Federation. In 1889, she was asked to write a review for *The Pall Mall Gazette* on *The Secret Doctrine*, the seminal work by Helena Petrovna Blavatsky. She sought an interview with its author and met

Blavatsky in Paris. Blavatsky was one of the founder members of the theosophical movement along with Henry Steel Olcott and William Quan Judge. The society was set up to promote the comparative study of philosophy, religion and science. The society described itself as 'an unsectarian body of seekers after Truth, who endeavour to promote Brotherhood and strive to serve humanity'.

Besant joined the Theosophical Society and soon became a leading lecturer and author on theosophical subjects. She published a number of books including *Thought Forms* (with C.W. Leadbeater) in 1901 and *Esoteric Christianity* in 1905. While president of the Theosophical Society, Besant was based at its headquarters in Adyar, India. She became involved in the struggle for Indian self-determination and helped launch the Home Rule League in 1914. In the late 1920s, Besant travelled to the United States with her protégé Jiddu Krishnamurti, who she hailed as the new World Teacher and incarnation of Buddha. Although Krishnamurti distanced himself from theosophy in 1929, Besant remained loyal to him. After her death, Krishnamurti, Aldous Huxley, Guido

Ferrando, and Rosalind Rajagopal built the Besant Hill School of Happy Valley in her honour. Besant's many pamphlets include *The Gospel of Christianity and the Gospel of Freethought* (1883), *Life, Death, and Immortality* (1886), *Why I Do Not Believe in God* (1887), and *Theosophy and the Search for Happiness* (1918).

The Place of Religion
in National Life by
Annie Besant (1917)

If I tried to say what is the place of religion in National life, and if I answered or defined that position, I should certainly say that its place is everywhere. No religion is a true religion unless it permeates the whole life of a man, and a Nation cannot be called religious unless it be inspired in the whole of its activities by religious feeling, religious thought, religious action. But that very general definition would hardly meet the views of those who have come here to listen to something more precise, although really not more accurate. I want, if I can, this evening, to try to show you to some extent not only the necessity of religion in the life of a Nation, but also something of what history has taught us of the effect of religion on National life. Some of you may remember reading, with relation to the want of religion, a rather interesting, because a very significant sentence of a great writer: 'The times of atheism have always been civil times' - times of peace, times with small excitement, times in which the life of a Nation was running smoothly though perhaps somewhat sluggishly for if we look widely at history, we shall see that, when a Nation has become very wealthy, very prosperous, very luxurious, then the intellectual and the spiritual elements in that Nation tend to become overborne by the physical and the material, and so we notice in history that those 'civil times' of which Bacon spoke, and which, he said, were characteristic of atheistic thought, have been times followed very shortly by National decay.

Nations growing over-wealthy and over-luxurious tend to lose acuteness of intellect, and still more to lose the keenness of spiritual insight. It has always been said by the great religious teachers of mankind that it is necessary for spiritual progress that a man should be self-controlled, that he should be abstemious as regards the luxuries of life, that he should be master of his body, and not permit his body to be master of mind and spirit. There is always a danger when things go too easily with a Nation. As a poet once said, 'when wealth accumulates, men decay.' A certain amount of hardness is wanted in the development of a healthy National life, and one who studied this side of man with some care put a curious proposition, which is by no means without a kernel of truth. Speaking of war, and saying, rather rashly, not being a prophet, that we were not likely to have much war at the stage of civilisation that mankind has reached, James said that Nations would require some substitute for war, that war brought out qualities of courage, of strength, of endurance, of power to resist hardship and to live without the luxuries of life; and what, he asked, in a civilisation which tends to grow soft and enervating, can we have which will take the place of war as a strengthener of man? He went on to point out the possibility that voluntary poverty might take the place of war - not the forced poverty that ruins the body, makes weak the will and breaks the heart, not the miserable poverty that we see around us in every civilised Nation, but a voluntary choice of a simple and non-luxurious life, a poverty embraced, as a great Christian Saint embraced it, voluntarily undergone and not compulsorily endured - James thought that that might take the place perhaps of war, after war had become impossible for civilised people, and that it would supply the mental stimulus which goes with a simple and abstemious life, and prevents the luxuries of life from tending to mental, spiritual, and even physical decay.

Looking then at that historical fact, we have seen that with the decay of thought and the decay of religion, a Nation tends to become over-luxurious and so strikes the knell of its own coming death. We may look around the European civilisation and see that this terrible outbreak of war has perhaps rescued Europe from being over-luxurious on the one side, and oblivious of the terrible and brutalising poverty upon the other. It has made a call to many of the higher qualities of self-denial and self-sacrifice, the giving up of all that people say makes life worth living, and to the great ideal that makes man feel that he has risen above the animal, that there is something greater than physical life, something nobler than physical enjoyment. So we find, looking at religion, that it is essentially an aspiration to the higher Self. The essence of religion, that which is common to all religions, is the aspiration of the heart towards God, the searching for God and God's answer to the searching. Looking at human nature, we find that the thirst for God, as one great Hebrew writer called it, is an integral part of the human constitution.

Many people, mistaking what religion means

and seeing the quarrels, the controversies, the hatreds, the strifes that have risen out of it, say that we should be better without religion, and that we should throw religion aside, for it breeds mischief, dissension, quarrel and hatred. But it is useless to say to mankind: 'Throw religion aside.' Man is so constituted in his inner nature that there is an inextinguishable thirst within him which nothing but the knowledge of God can satisfy. For a time, it may be, especially in youth, he is easily satisfied with the outer things of life, but when the difficulties of life have to be met, when the laws of life are experienced, when sorrow wrings the heart and disappointment breaks the courage, then it is that in man awakens the thirst for God, and it was truly said by St. Augustine that 'man can never find rest until he finds rest in Thee'. That was once put very beautifully by an English poet, George Herbert, who was mystic in his thought, quaint in his poetry. He put his thought long after St. Augustine, and he threw it into poetical form:

> *When God at first made man,*
> *Having a glass of blessings standing by,*

'Let us,' said He, 'pour on him all we can;
Let the world's riches, which dispersed lie,
Contract into a span.

So strength first made a way;
Then beauty flowed; then wisdom, honour, pleasure;
When almost all was out, God made a stay;
Perceiving that alone, of all His treasure,
Rest in the bottom lay.

'For if I should,'said He,
'Bestow this jewel also on My creature,
He would adore my gifts instead of me,
And rest in nature, not the God of nature -
So both should losers be.

'Yet let him keep the rest -
But keep them with repining restlessness -
Let him be rich and weary; that, at least,
If goodness lead him not, yet weariness
May toss him to my breast.'

The thought there is at once beautiful and true. Man's progress is made by disappointments. Just as a mother coaxes a child to walk by holding up some glittering object so that the child strives to crawl and then walk to reach it, so does God play with His children. God dangles in front of them some shining object. 'Come,' He practically says, 'and take this toy,' and the child strives after it and exerts its strength in striving: it is wealth, or power, or fame, or pleasure; but whatever it is, the only value of it is in the effort to reach it, and not in the holding after it is won. A man becomes wealthy, but his wealth burdens him; he finds pleasure, but pleasure cloys him; he grasps power, and he finds his pillow full of thorns; he seeks satisfaction in one thing after another, and everything breaks to pieces in his hands, and turns, like the fruit of that fabled tree in Milton's Hell, into ashes in his mouth; and then at last, after many disappointments, having gained value of the striving in the development of his mind and in the power of his emotions, then at last, wearied with all worldly toys, he turns to God alone, and finding in the divinity within him the power of answer to the divinity without, then and then only is his aspiration satisfied, and he finds his rest in Him who is verily himself. And so all the great struggles of man, whatever they may be, are really struggles to find Brahman, who is bliss. He seeks happiness: he does well; it is a true instinct although his methods are mistaken; inasmuch as the very heart of the universe is love and joy, inasmuch as God is love and God is bliss, that yearning after happiness felt by every child of man is really an aspiration after God; that is an impulse to progress, that is a spur to all true endeavour; and so the very essence of religion is the motive power of evolution, and a Nation, as well as an individual, can only progress by the power of the Spirit within. That is true of religion as a whole. Any special religion has its value in its partaking of that aspiration after God. If you take the separate religions, then you will find that in a Nation's life, the religion by which the Nation has been built up stamps its civilisation and guides its polity.

Look over the great religions of the world, as we have known them in the so-called historical times, and you will find that each type of civilisation differs as the religion on which that civilisation is built gradually shapes and moulds it to its own likeness. If you take Hinduism, the oldest of the Aryan religions, you find that the whole of the

Hindu polity is built up on its religion. The whole of the mighty civilisation of the past is the outcome of its religion. You have not only the Vedas and the Upanishads, showing a mighty intellect and giving you a splendid philosophy, a marvellous spirituality; you have also a set of books that you know as the Dharma Shastras, the law which lays down the conduct of the people and gives a definite line of evolution which the people should follow. Similarly, you find that side by side, penetrated with the religion, you have the knowledge, the science of the old Hindus. You find that within the six great Darshanas,[1] and four of them are practically given to science. If you take Sankhya,[2] Patanjali,[3] Nyaya,[4] Vyakarana,[5] what have you there but science of the deepest and the most splendid description? Some of you may have seen that remarkable book by Brijendranath Seal[6] on the science of the old Hindus, on which I am writing in New India. You find in those conceptions of Sãnkhya, conceptions of modern science precisely, definitely and accurately voiced, with a depth of understanding, of power, of abstract thought that has never been outdone in the modern world.

You find the very foundations of modern science laid down there as part of the philosophy of Hindu antiquity.

Of all philosophy, the ancient Hindu told us that all philosophy has for its end to put an end to pain. Ask any of the great philosophies what is its object ? 'To put an end to pain', is the answer; and then there comes another significant verse, that you might as well try to roll up the akasha[7] like leather as to give happiness to man without the knowledge of God. So you find that, whether in philosophy or in science, this mighty Hindu religion has moulded Indian life, has inspired Indian thought, has stimulated Indian action; for you must not forget that I have not time to dwell upon it in any detail, not only with regard to religion as such, but also the right conduct of man, as politics. Some of the other books dealt with the constitution of States, with the relation of the citizens to the State, and shaped and moulded the lives of the people; and I do not know that anywhere, in the ancient or modern world, you will find a single religion that so touches human life at every point as Hinduism has done, whether in the conduct of the individual or as shaping the larger life of the Nation. In Hinduism, as in another Eastern faith familiar to you - the religion of the Hebrews - you will find that all that was wanted to make the life of the people healthy and happy came to them with the authority of religion. You know it so well with regard to your own religion. You know how often the laws of sanitation, of hygiene, of cleanliness, of being scrupulously careful with water, with food, and with drink, and so on, come in as part of the religious duty of man. It was the same with the Hebrews.

I do not suppose that you have studied very much the old laws of Moses, but if you have, you will find that in those laws, meant for the guidance of the Hebrew Nation, are laid down particulars of the daily life of the people that may often remind you of the laws laid down by your own great teachers. To a man of the ancient day, there was no division in life between religion and the whole life of man. If he was healthy, his religion taught him how to become healthy. If his town was sanitary and well looked after, he was obeying the precepts of his religion that came to him with that external authority. The difficulty you will have in reading the

Mosaic books, is that they are mixed up with crudities, because the Jewish Nation was not in those early days a highly educated nor an artistic Nation. You will come across phrases so curious, and occasional comments so immoral, that you are apt to overlook the value of the other parts of the Mosaic teachings. There are some absurd statements, some immoral statements as regards women; others made a duty of persecution: if a man did not follow the law of the Hebrew deity, then he was to be slain. Those are blots that belong rather to the nature of the people, I think, than to the teachings of their prophet, just as you will find occasionally in the laws of Manu[8] phrases which are impossible to accept as coming from the real writer of those valuable laws of a Nation. All ancient books are subject to that difficulty. You must use intelligence in reading them, and you must learn to discriminate between the words of the Sage and that which is very often the gloss of a later commentator who, in order to serve the purpose of the moment, wrote into the original manuscript something which was useful for the time, as he thought, but was utterly out of accord with the ancient teaching that he injured and lowered in the minds of the thoughtful.

You may turn from Hinduism and take other religions which, one after another, had a National life based upon them. The second great religion that followed on Hinduism, going further west along the border of the Mediterranean, in Egypt, Cyprus, etc., was a religion peculiarly scientific in its nature. The Egyptian religion was based on the knowledge of the physical world and of the physical body of man. Very much of your own Hatha Yoga[9] is closely connected with a similar form of Yoga among the Egyptians. They studied the body of man in relation to the body of the universe, and found out the relations between the parts of the human body and the larger parts of the great organism of the solar system. Those of you who have studied the deeper thoughts of Hatha Yoga will find that the line of thought and practice is familiar in many of the Tantras.[10] It almost seems as though Hinduism were the parent religion of the religions of the West, as the Aryan ethnological stock is the parent of all the emigrations that went out westward. You find in that Mediterranean and

Egyptian civilisation one more type of civilisation moulded entirely by the religion of the people. You find the Science that made the precision of Egypt the marvel of the world, and made their priests able to perform so-called miracles, which were simply the utilisation of some of the generally unknown laws of nature to produce results which, as it were, convinced the ignorant, not by appealing to the mind, but by dazzling the senses.

When you turn from that to the better known civilisation of Persia, you find there in the religion of Zoroaster the essential characteristic of purity underlying everything, a civilisation largely based on agriculture, on cultivation of land, and side by side with that, a similar development of astronomy and astrology, so that all agricultural operations, as is also seen in India, were arranged on astrological calculations, and the beginnings of every great season of the year were marked by festivals of the planets, the sun and the moon. Right through that civilisation this idea of purity runs, and of the relation between the planetary bodies and man. You must be pure in thought, in word, in deed. You must be pure as far as your houses are concerned, as far as your towns are concerned, as far as your rivers are concerned. No Zoroastrian would have allowed rivers to be polluted, as they are polluted today in England by factories that pour all refuse into them and make them sources of poison instead of sources of health. Everywhere the law of purity ruled in that ancient Persia, with the result of a splendid, healthy, virile people, a long-lived Nation, because they obeyed the religious law which, carried out in life, gives health, strength and vigour.

But when you come to the next great civilisation and its religion, you come into an entirely different atmosphere. It was the religion and civilisation of Greece. There the keynote was Beauty; not spirituality of thought as in Hinduism, not knowledge of science as in Egypt, not purity of life as in Persia, but beauty of life. When you think of Greece you always think of beauty. The most exquisite buildings come from her architecture. The grandest statues are imitations of her sculpture. The whole education of the Greeks was an education in beauty. The results of that on the life of the Nation were striking. The Greeks were surrounded by objects of beauty. Their city was full of architecture, the streets were the decorations of the capital. The Greek was the Nation of the most beautiful forms of humanity, because of the influence of beauty on the mind and the life of the people. Everything that the Greek used was artistic: his domestic vessels, his lamps, the things in which he carried water or cooked food were all beautiful, and the result of that was that the people were beautiful. The mother, surrounded with lovely objects, gave birth to children moulded into harmony and beauty by the beauty that surrounded her. That was the great teaching of Greece - the value of beauty in human life, and not only in outer objects created by the artist but in the beauty of language used by the poet, by the dramatist, by the philosopher. The form side of life had its perfection in Greece, and the whole religion of Greece was a religion of beauty which shaped the type of its civilisation.

That was succeeded in Rome by Christianity: an entirely different civilisation grew up as the life of the Nations of Europe. If you seek what was wanting in the elder days, you will find that what was left out was the sense of the value of the individual. You know how in Hinduism man is not an individual man: he is the man, the wife, and the child; it is the family and not the individual, isolated human being - a far more perfect conception, the conception on which the State hereafter will be modelled. The conception of the family life extended to the life of the Nation, just as you find Manu telling people to look on the poor, the younger and the uneducated as children; to look on all equals as brothers and sisters; to look on all elders as fathers and mothers. That was the idea of ancient India as regards social gradation, and the whole caste system is built up on that idea of elders, equals and youngers. But that omitted a very essential part which was needed for the future evolution of man, and that essential part was given in the religion of Christianity. The doctrines of Christianity, you must have often noticed have lost very much that belonged to the other religions of the world. The earlier Christianity lost the great doctrine of reincarnation, and so there was a danger of its losing the doctrine of immortality, though men clung to it against all reason and argument by the intuition that saved it. But you find in the history of Christendom that it is man's own soul that is the supreme matter of importance. There grew up a strong individuality. There is no use in objecting to a fact of that kind which is necessary for human evolution. It was necessary to have a strong individual, and that could only be developed by effort. You have in Christendom a civilisation, not only individualistic but combative, one man striving against another, every man fighting for his own hand. It is not only a question of physical war; but it is a question of social war, it is a question of class war, and you do not find all those wars developed anywhere as you find them developed in Christendom - evil you may be inclined to think, short-sightedly - but it is not. It is working to a greater good. The example of Christ was sure in the long run to correct this necessary fault in the Christian teaching, not found in Himself but found in His Apostles. You must remember that Christianity was made by St. Paul far more than it was made by Christ Himself. It was St. Paul who gave a dogmatic side to Christianity and made religion into a Church - a very, very different thing. Gradually, however, it was inevitable that the example of Christ should correct the faults of the civilisation by the example of true self-sacrifice. You have that corrective in the teaching as well as the example of Christ.

'He that is greatest is he that doth serve.' 'Behold,' He told His Apostles, 'I am among you as he that serveth.' Out of that came gradually the idea that strength was made for service and not for oppression, and that which you call in Christendom public spirit, patriotism, love of country, altruism - all these were virtues that flowered out of that competitive system which had developed the strength necessary for the next step forward in human life; and strength linked to service is the ultimate lesson of Christianity.

So looking over all these, we find in these different religions that each moulds the life of its own Nation, and that the spirit of the religion shapes the body of the National life. How does that affect us in India, where all the great religions are now found ? Does it not strike you that in the ruling of Ishvara in His world there must be some reason why this Motherland of the Aryan race has living on her soil all the great religions which have been as it were born out of her womb? The Hindu here has his religion as active, as living, as compelling as ever. The Musalmans[11] are here the next greatest Indian community. The Parsi[12] are here not very numerous, it is true, but are influencing the Indian life by that commercial life which they had developed strongly by their wealth, by their enterprise and by their knowledge. Christians are here and in western and southern India there are great Christian communities that date back at least to the fifth and sixth centuries of the Christian era perhaps even to the second century A.D. So that there are hereditary Christians here, as much as most of you are hereditary Hindus. They have a place here, not as aliens but as children of the soil. We see the religion of Buddhism, founded here by Lord Buddha Himself, and spread on to the other adjacent countries. We find all the great religions on this mother soil of India. How will they inevitably affect her National life?

It is clear that as the outer ways are different, the outer customs are different, the outer dogmas are different, we must look to the uniting power of the religions in the spirit of Religion more than in the outer forms. I might show you that, even in the outer forms, they are so closely welded together that anyone who knows them intimately could make parallel lines showing how in ceremonies, rites and customs, they reproduce each other. Let me remind you only of one case. You all know that when your relatives pass away you perform shraddha.[13] You know the essential objects used in the shraddha ceremony. You must have a material object, and you have it in a Pinda,[14] and later in water. You must have a word of power - the Mantra. Without the Mantra what shraddha could be performed? You must have certain gestures - Mudra,[15] the fingers form a part of the ceremony; the whole of these are more or less familiar. Only some of the younger men, who have not grown wise, think that this is all superstition.

Take for a moment the Roman Catholic ceremony, which is more closely allied to Hinduism than is Protestantism. It is no use converting a Hindu to Christianity. If you have the whole thing in your religion in a very perfect form, why should you take it in another form from another religion? The Roman Catholic teaches that there is the other side of death, and Roman Catholics perform for those who have passed onwards what you may call the Christian shraddha - Mass for the dead. The idea is exactly the same as for Hindus. You perform your shraddha in order to help those who have gone, onwards through the stage of Kamaloka[16] to Pitrloka.[17] The Roman Catholic performs his Mass for the dead in order that his beloved may pass onwards from Purgatory or Kamaloka on to a happier life of Paradise - not rice in his case but bread, not water but wine. You notice there that you have two things, solid and liquid, used in two religious ceremonies with the same object.

Then, you find that there are certain words pronounced, and pronounced in the Latin tongue - not in the tongue of the people, but in their sacred tongue. I have often heard young men say: 'Why should I use Sanskrit words if I do not understand them?' Because words are sounds, and sounds produce vibrations, and if you change the sounds you change the vibrations, and the sounds are meant to produce certain vibrations that will affect the sukshma sharira[18] of man. A Roman Catholic pronounces his mantra in Latin. He pronounces the Latin form and produces the necessary vibrations from the sounds of the words. He also makes his gesture - the Sign of the Cross - using it over consecrated bread, using it over the cup where the sacred liquid is. You must be very blind if you do not realise that with a little difference of outer sign and not of real essence of meaning, these two ceremonies are exactly the same. They use the same methods and they have the same objects. In the one case they are helped by beings you speak of as Devas, and in the other case as Angels. The meaning of Devas is Shining Ones - you only use the Hindu form of description. The Roman Catholic calls them Angels and not Devas, but the meaning is the same.

Every spirit in a human being is the spirit of God, and there is no other source of life; if you realise that you have the same difficulties, the same troubles, that you are born and die and are followed in your death by similar love and similar effort on the part of your neighbour whose outer name is not the same as yours; you begin to see the essence of religion, you begin to realise that man, in yearning after God and in searching after God, wears different garments, but the emotion and the endeavour are the same, and that Religion should become a binding power and not a separative force.

Then, you may begin to realise that these many religions of the world on Indian soil are meant to bring together into one mighty power all the powers of the world. Hinduism brings its jewel and Christianity, Zoroastrianism and Buddhism bring their own jewels, different in colour but alike in their preciousness. You will begin to understand that the Indian Nation of the future is not to be a Nation of one single religion only, but to embody the very essence of all religions; that it will have in it the philosophy of Hinduism, the purity of Zoroastrianism, the love and tenderness of Buddhism, the self-sacrifice of Christianity. All these exquisite qualities, coming from the one Brotherhood of Teachers, and spreading abroad among this mighty Nation, will bring a completeness of perfection that a single religion, however noble and perfect, could never give, and you will realise how full of insight and truth were the words of the great Swami Vivekananda,[19] that a variety of religions was a gain and not a loss. Every view of God is added to the views already held, and so, however infinite the perfection of God Himself, more and more knowledge of that perfect Being will come to India through the many religions born on its soil and nourished by itself.

1. Darsana is the auspicious sight of a deity or a holy person. The term also refers to six orthodox schools of Hindu philosophy and their literature on spirituality and salvation.

2. Samkhya or Sankhya is one of the six major philosophies of Hinduism. Samkhya, meaning 'enumeration', defines the many layers of human existence. It enumerates the components of mind, body and spirit, from the densest material of the physical body to the subtle, etheric elements of the mind and consciousness. It can be regarded as a plan or blueprint of the human being.

3. Patanjali was a sage in Hinduism, thought to be the author of a number of Sanskrit works. The greatest of these are the Yoga Sutras, classical texts of Hindu philosophy.

4. Nyaya literally means 'rules', 'method' or 'judgment'. It is also the name of one of the six orthodox (astika) schools of Hinduism. This school's most significant contributions to Indian philosophy were the systematic development of the theory of logic, methodology, and its treatises on epistemology.

5. Vyakaraṇa, meaning 'explanation, analysis', refers to one of the six ancient Vedangas, ancillary science connected with the Vedas, which are scriptures in Hinduism. Vyakaraṇa is the study of Sanskrit.

6. Sir Brajendra Nath Seal (3 September 1864 - 3 December 1938) was a renowned Bengali Indian humanist philosopher specialising in comparative religion and the philosophy of science.

7. In Vedantic Hinduism, Akasha means the basis and essence of all things in the material world; the first element created.

8. Manusmṛti, also called the Manava-Dharmasastra or Laws of Manu is an ancient legal text. It was one of the first Sanskrit texts to be translated into English and was used to formulate Hindu law by the British colonial government.

9. Hatha Yoga is a branch of yoga. The Sanskrit word 'haṭha' means literally 'force', so alluding to the system of physical techniques and postures.

10. Tantras ('Looms' or 'Weavings') are the numerous and varied scriptures pertaining to any of several esoteric traditions rooted in Hindu and Buddhist philosophy.

11. The Musalmans are Indian muslims.

12. Parsi, also spelled Parsee, are followers in India of the Persian prophet Zoroaster.

13. Sraddha or Shraaddha is a Sanskrit word meaning any act performed with all sincerity and faith. In the Hindu religion, it is the ritual that one performs to pay homage to one's ancestors, especially to one's dead parents. It also can be thought of as a 'day of remembrance'.

14. Piṇḍas are balls of cooked rice and barley flour mixed with ghee and black sesame seeds offered to ancestors during Hindu funeral rites (Antyesti) and ancestor worship (Sraddha).

15. Mudra is a Sanskrit word meaning 'seal', 'mark', or 'gesture'. It describes a symbolic or ritual gesture in Hinduism, Jainism and Buddhism.

16. Kamaloka is a semi-material plane, subjective and invisible to humans, where disembodied 'personalities', the astral forms, called Kama-rupa remain until they fade from it.

17. Pitrloka, in Hinduism, the place where dead ancestors reside.

18. Sukshma sharira or the 'subtle body' is the body of the mind and the vital energies, which keeps the physical body alive.

19. Swami Vivekananda (12 January 1863 - 4 July 1902), born Narendranath Datta, was an Indian Hindu monk and a chief disciple of the 19th-century Indian mystic Ramakrishna. He was a key figure in the introduction of the Indian philosophies of Vedanta and Yoga to the Western world and is credited with raising interfaith awareness, bringing Hinduism to the status of a major world religion during the late 19th Century.

www.ingramcontent.com/pod-product-compliance
Lightning Source LLC
Chambersburg PA
CBHW021129080526
44587CB00012B/1202